Measure It with Math!

MEASURING HEIGHT

Anne O'Daly

PowerKiDS press

Published in 2024 by The Rosen Publishing Group, Inc.
2544 Clinton Street, Buffalo, NY 14224

Portions of this work were originally authored by Chris Woodford and published as *Height*.
All new material this edition authored by Anne O'Daly.

Children's Publisher: Anne O'Daly

Design Manager: Keith Davis

Picture Manager: Sophie Mortimer

Picture credits:

Key: t = top, tr = top right, b = bottom

Front Cover: Shutterstock: tl, S. J. Allen l, Marco La Melia tr, Vixit r.

Interior: iStock: Nirian 26; Shutterstock: ABB Photo 23, Africa Studio 5, Volodymyr Bburdiak 8, Apiwan Borrikonratchata 12, Tomasz Czajkowski 27t, elbud 4, Jason Finn 17r, Imfoto 17l, Eric Isselée 13, Ivaylo Ivanov 28l, Gitsalak Karalak 15, Stanislav Khokholkov 19l, Taras Kushnir 1, 22, Luis Louro 28-29, Vadim Martvnenko 6, John Milnes 14, New Africa 19r, nortongo 11, RedStock 7, Alexey Seafarer 21, StevanZZ 9, Tish1 10, Vixit 27b, Martin Voeller 24.

Cataloging-in-Publication Data

Names: O'Daly, Anne.
Title: Measuring height / Anne O'Daly.
Description: New York : Powerkids Press, 2024. | Series: Measure it with math! | Includes glossary and index.
Identifiers: ISBN 9781642827798 (pbk.) | ISBN 9781642827804 (library bound) | ISBN 9781642827811 (ebook)
Subjects: LCSH: Measurement--Juvenile literature.| Weights and measures--Juvenile literature. | Mathematics--Juvenile literature.
Classification: LCC QC90.6 O34 2024 | DDC 530.8--dc23

Manufactured in the United States of America

CPSIA Compliance Information: Batch #CSPK24. For further information contact Rosen Publishing at 1-800-237-9932.

Contents

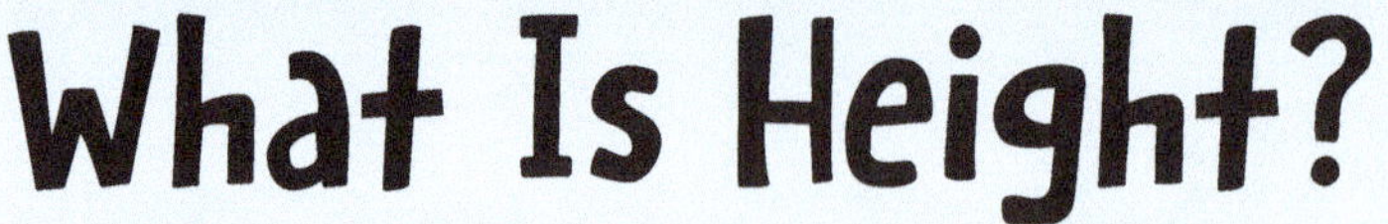

What Is Height?

How tall are you? Who is the tallest person in your family? Who is the shortest? We use these words to talk about height. We measure the height of people. We also measure the height of buildings and mountains.

Touching the Sky

Many big cities have tall buildings. They are called skyscrapers. The Empire State Building is in New York City. It is one of the world's most famous skyscrapers. It reaches 1,250 feet (381 meters) into the air. It would take 330 children, standing on one another's shoulders, to reach the top!

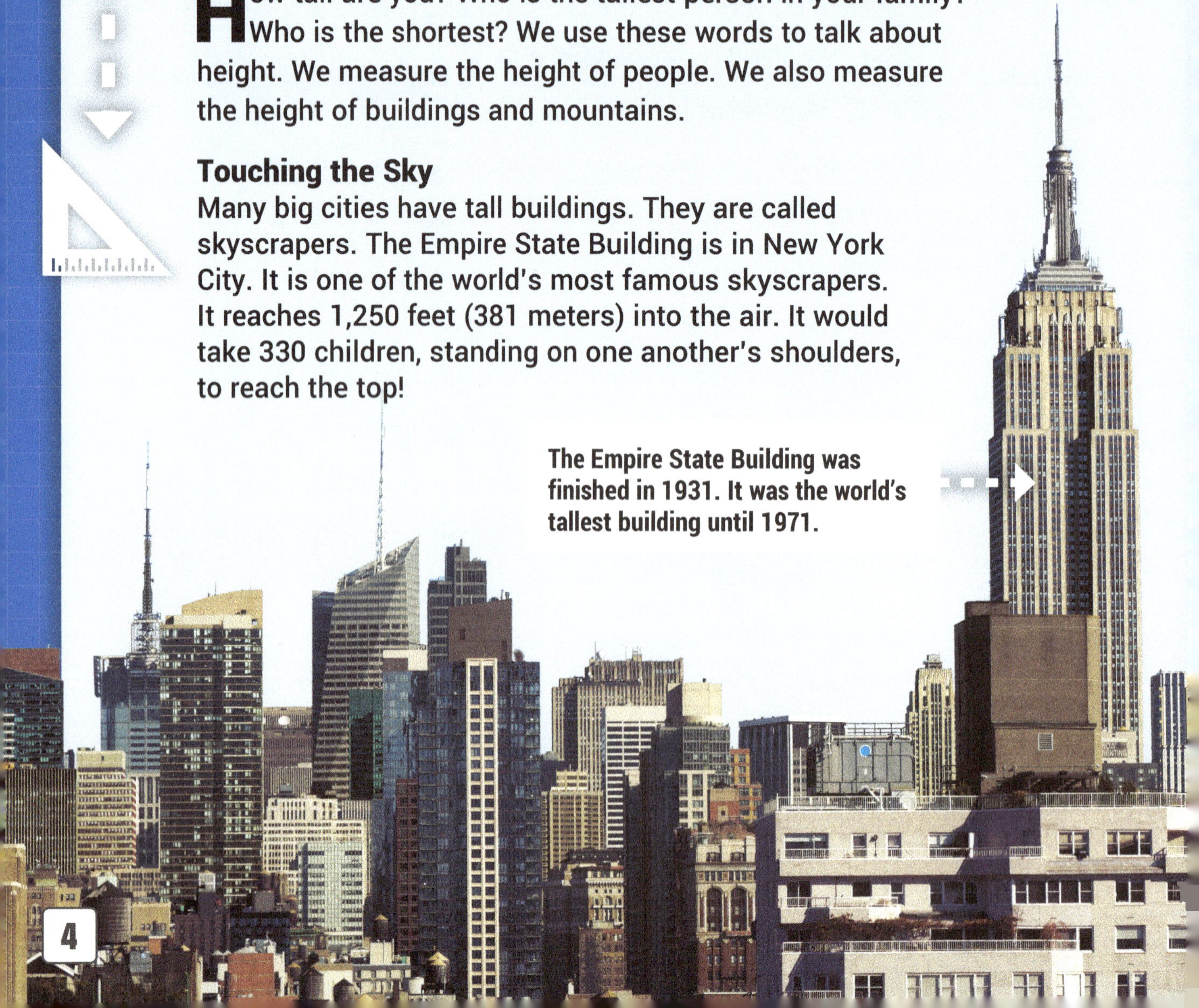

The Empire State Building was finished in 1931. It was the world's tallest building until 1971.

TALLER IN THE MORNING

You are a little taller when you wake up than when you go to bed. During the day, your weight squeezes your body down. It squashes the bones in your back. When you lie in bed, the bones stretch out again.

Height and Length

Height is a measurement. It tells us how tall something is. The height of the Empire State Building is how far it goes up into the air.

Length is a measurement along the ground. Suppose we could lie a building on its side. We could measure its height by measuring how long it stretched down the street. Measuring height is the same as measuring length or distance.

FACT

The world's tallest building is the Burj Khalifa in Dubai. It is over 2,716.5 feet (828 m) high. That's twice as tall as the Empire State Building.

How Can We Measure Height?

Different tools help us measure height. We can measure shorter distances with a ruler or tape measure. We measure height in the same way that we measure length. But we have to point the ruler upward rather than sideways.

Rulers and Tape Measures

Rulers are stiff and have straight edges. They have different units marked along either side. A school ruler is usually 12 inches (30 cm) long. Rulers are good for measuring small items, like books.

This person is measuring a piece of wood with a tape measure.

TRY THIS

HOW TALL ARE YOU?

Find a flat part of the floor next to a wall. Take off your shoes and stand against the wall. Place a book on top of your head. Hold the book with one hand. Use the other hand to make a small pencil mark on the wall just under the book. Ask an adult's permission first! Use a tape measure or ruler to measure the distance from the ground to the pencil mark. The measurement is your height.

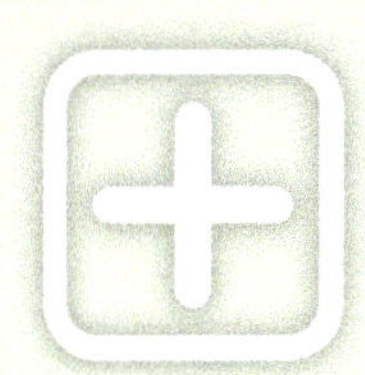

FACT

You can measure height with a smartphone. An app measures the distance between two points. It can measure short objects and tall objects.

Long Rulers

Yardsticks and metersticks are long rulers. A yardstick measures 3 feet. A meterstick is 1 meter long. For longer distances, we use a tape measure. Tape measures are bendy. They can be any length, from a few feet to hundreds of feet.

Rulers and tape measures have lines and numbers marked along the side. The lines show the measurements. These lines are called the scale.

Yards, Feet, and Inches

Some measurements are in yards, feet, and inches. These are called Imperial measurements. They are commonly used in the United States.

We could use a ruler to measure a small bird. The bird is 6 inches tall. A tape measure could show that an adult is 6 feet tall. The height of a house might be 6 yards.

Animals come in many shapes and sizes. Here are the average heights of some animals.

Animal	Height
Fly	¼ inch
Lizard	1 to 2 inches
Cat	1 foot
Dog	6 inches to 3 feet
Adult human	5 to 6 feet
Horse	5 to 7 feet
Giraffe	15 to 19 feet

A house's height can be measured in yards.

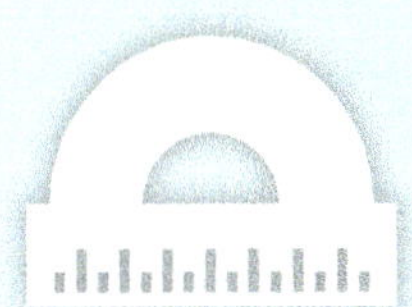

Units

The house, the person, and the bird all measure 6 units. But the bird is smaller than the person. The person is smaller than the house. The number six means something different each time.

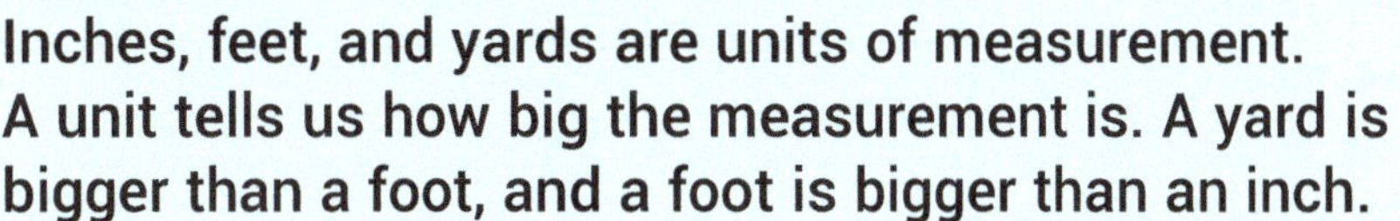

Inches, feet, and yards are units of measurement. A unit tells us how big the measurement is. A yard is bigger than a foot, and a foot is bigger than an inch.

Make It Metric

In other parts of the world, people measure heights with different units. These units include millimeters, centimeters, and meters. This way of measuring is called the metric system.

Metric Measurements

The metric system works in tens, hundreds, and thousands. There are 100 centimeters in 1 meter. There are 1,000 meters in 1 kilometer.

TRY THIS

MEASURE YOURSELF

Find a tape measure that has inches on one side and centimeters on the other. Measure your height in the same way as on page 7. First measure in feet and inches, and then in meters and centimeters. The measurements will look different, but they are the same. Your height is the same, even if you use different units to measure it.

Rulers and tape measures are often marked with either imperial or metric units. Some have both. They have inches along one side and centimeters on the other side.

CHANGING HEIGHTS

We can change measurements from feet and inches into meters and centimeters, and the other way around. This table, right, shows some height measurements in both imperial and metric units.

- 1 inch = about 2.5 cm
- 1 foot, or 12 inches = about 30 cm
- 1 cm = about 0.4 inch
- 1 meter, or 100 cm = 3 feet 3 inches, or 39 inches

Rulers often show both the imperial and metric scales.

How to Estimate Height

Measuring someone's height with a ruler or tape measure is called a measurement. If you've been careful and accurate, a measurement is usually exact. But there are other ways you can measure height. You don't always need to have equipment.

Taller or Shorter

Sometimes we can figure out height by looking. This is called an estimate. If you know your own height, you can probably guess how tall your friends are. Some will be taller. Others will be shorter.

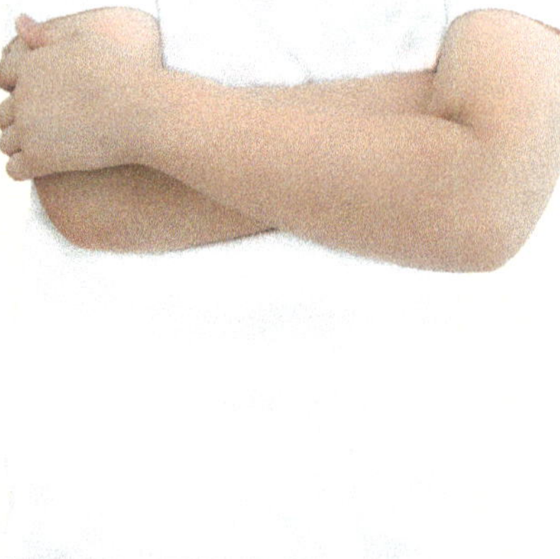

It's easiest to estimate the height of something if you have measured something else first. Suppose you have measured the height of a cat. Now imagine a dog standing next to the cat. You can probably estimate the height of the dog quite easily. But if you hadn't measured the cat, it would be more difficult.

TEST YOUR SKILLS

You can test your estimating skills like this. Estimate the height of something by comparing it. Then measure it. How close was your estimate to the measurement? If it was close, it was a good estimate. An estimate is not the same as a guess. With an estimate, we want to be as close as possible. With a guess, accuracy doesn't matter.

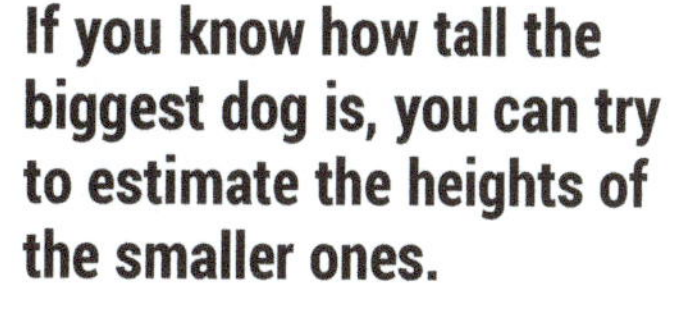

If you know how tall the biggest dog is, you can try to estimate the heights of the smaller ones.

Measuring Down

We measure height from the ground up. Mountains, buildings, and people have height. They stand up above the ground. Another kind of height goes down. That measurement is depth. We measure depth from the ground to the lowest point. We measure the depth of swimming pools, lakes, and underground caves. A swimming pool may be 3 feet to 6 feet (about 1 to 3 m) deep. That's easy to measure. An ocean is much deeper.

INTO THE DEEP

The average depth of the ocean is about 12,100 feet (3,688 m). The deepest part is in the Mariana Trench, which is in the Pacific Ocean near Japan. The Mariana Trench is 7 miles (11 km) deep. If we could lay it in a straight line along the ground, it would take about two hours to walk from one end to the other.

Scuba divers use special equipment to breathe. Without scuba gear, a person can only dive down about 100 feet (30 m).

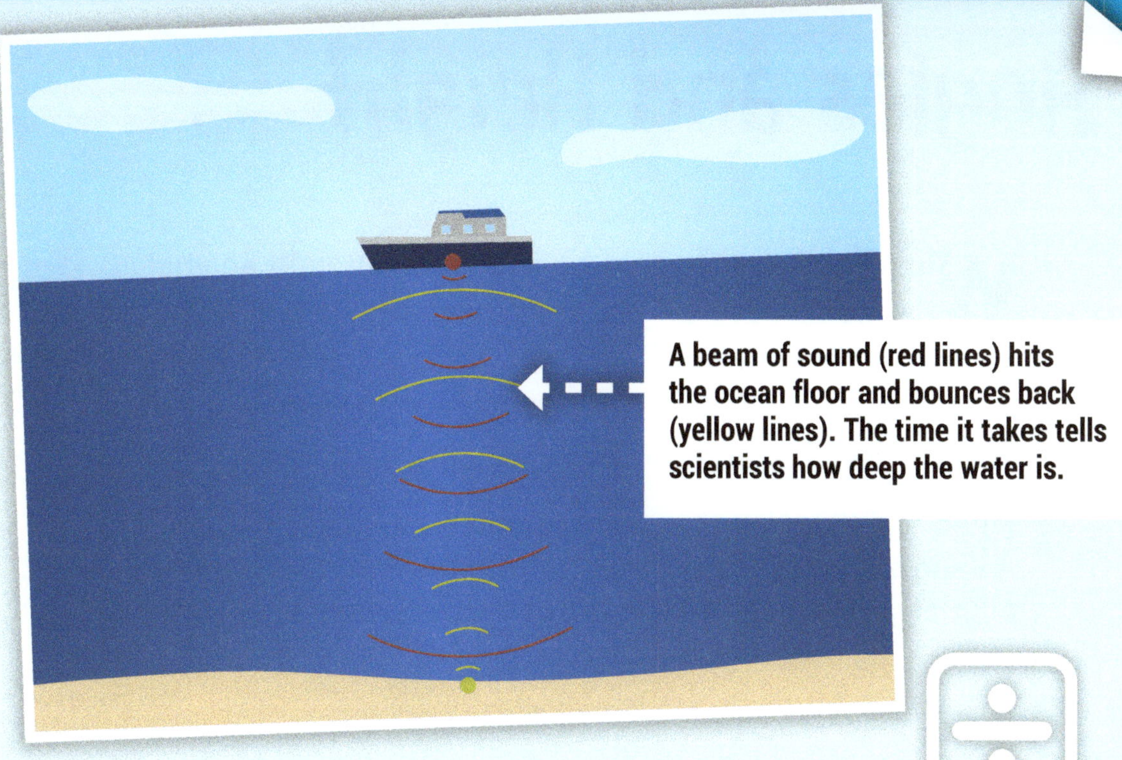

A beam of sound (red lines) hits the ocean floor and bounces back (yellow lines). The time it takes tells scientists how deep the water is.

How Deep Is the Ocean?

One way to measure the ocean's depth uses sound. Scientists send a beam of sound down from a ship. The sound hits the ocean floor and bounces back. The scientists measure how long it takes. That tells them how deep the water is.

Sailors used to lower a measuring rope over the ship's side. It had a heavy weight at the end to make it sink and marks along it to show distance. Once the weight hit the bottom, sailors could measure the distance to the ocean floor.

Angles and Height

When you measure your height, stand straight against the wall. That way, you are at your full height. If you stand away from the wall and lean back, you won't reach as high. The more you lean, the less high up the wall you reach. Try it and see!

When one thing leans against another, it makes an angle. An angle is the space between two lines that cross or meet. A small angle means there is not much space between the lines. A big angle means there is a lot of space.

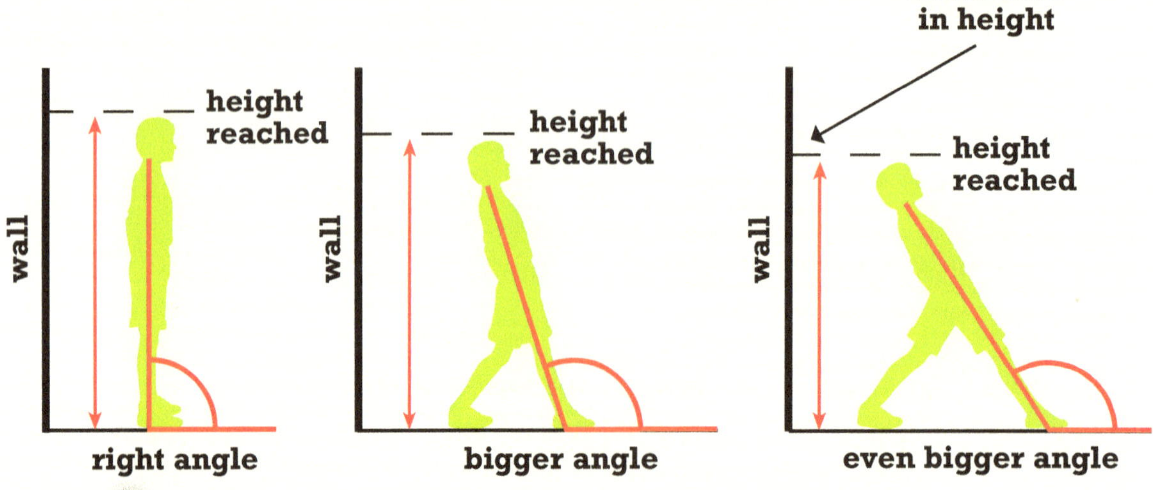

The more you lean against a wall, the bigger the angle you make and the less high up you reach.

TRY THIS

RIGHT ANGLES

A square corner is a special kind of angle. When two lines meet so that they make a boxlike corner, we call it a right angle. A right angle is like one corner of a square. Many of the things around us have right angles. Look around and see how many you can find.

These walls are at right angles to each other. Can you see any other right angles in this picture?

Measuring Angles

We measure height with a ruler or tape measure. The measurements are usually in inches and feet. Angles have their own units. They are called degrees. We use a special instrument called a protractor to measure angles. A protractor is like a curved ruler. It has degrees marked on it, rather than inches.

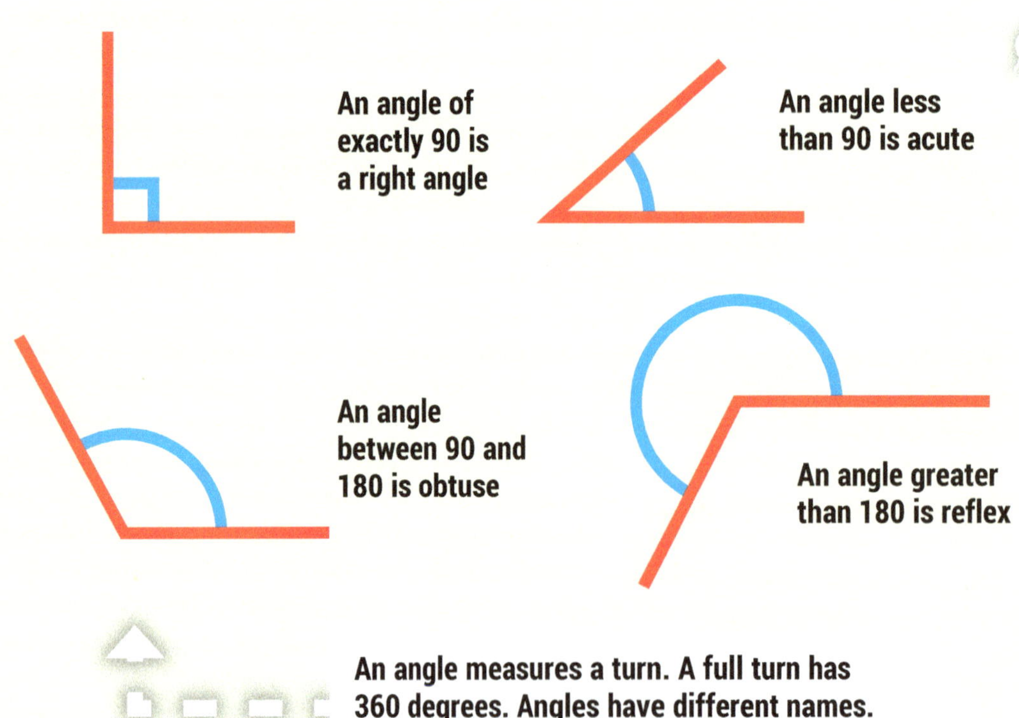

An angle measures a turn. A full turn has 360 degrees. Angles have different names.

TRY THIS

USING A PROTRACTOR

This is a protractor. It helps us measure angles. A protractor has a target mark in the center of its straight side. It has numbers around the outside. This is the scale. To measure an angle, put the target mark on the place where two lines meet. Line up the protractor so that one of the lines runs along the protractor's zero line. See where the other line meets the scale. Read the number on the scale to find the angle.

All at Sea

How do sailors know where they are at sea? Finding a position is called navigation. Modern ships use GPS technology to navigate. Before modern technology, sailors had other ways. During the day, they watched the sun move from east to west. At night, they looked at the moon and the stars.

USING A QUADRANT

A quadrant was a simple tool that sailors used to navigate. It had a curved side showing angles from 0 to 90 degrees. It had a small weight attached to its corner. A sailor would point the quadrant at an object in the sky and look along the straight edge. Wherever the plumb falls on the scale shows the angle. Using the angle and the time of day, the sailor could work out where the boat was.

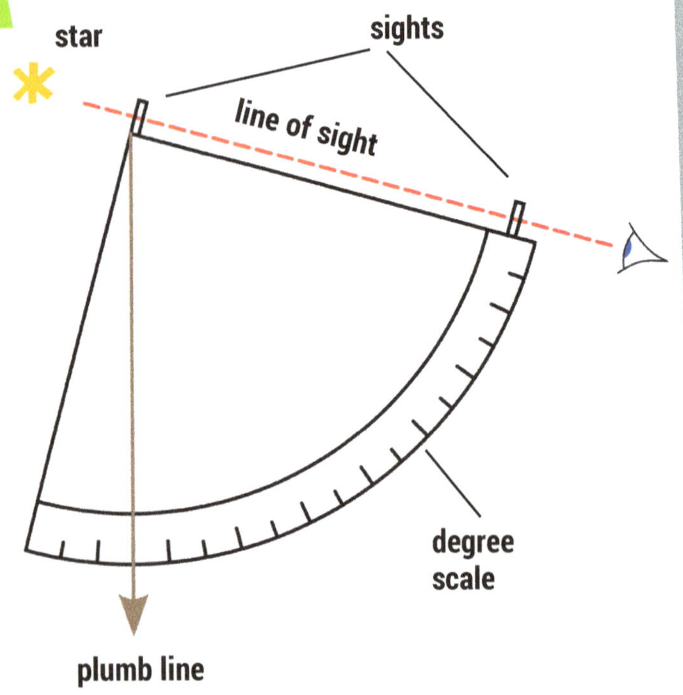

Sextants

Sailors could measure their position using a sextant. It was first used in the 1730s. A sextant is like a small telescope attached to a protractor (below). Sailors use sextants to measure the angle of the sun, moon, or a star above the horizon. With this angle, sailors can work out how far they are from the equator. Although sextants were invented a long time ago, sailors still use them today alongside modern methods.

Mountain High

Gravity is a force that pulls things toward the ground. It gets weaker as you climb a mountain, or at the top of a tall building. Gravity squeezes air to make air pressure. That makes the atmosphere, which has the air that we breathe. Gravity is weaker at the top of a mountain than at the bottom. Air pressure gets lower, too.

Air pressure gets lower as you climb up a mountain.

FLYING HIGH

An airplane's height above Earth is its altitude. Pilots need to know the altitude to help them fly the plane. They measure the airplane's height with an instrument called an altimeter. It works by measuring the air pressure. It uses the air pressure to figure out the altitude.

Airplanes always have altimeters on their control panels.

FACT

Mountain climbers who climb high mountains may need to take a supply of oxygen. The air is thinner at the top of a mountain, which makes it hard to breathe.

Climbing Higher

Low air pressure makes it harder to breathe. The higher up you go, the thinner the air gets. An instrument called a barometer measures air pressure. If you measure air pressure as you climb a mountain, you can figure out how high you are. Air pressure can also be used to measure the height of a building.

Habitat Heights

We share our planet with millions of different types, or species, of animals. Each species lives in its own particular place. The place where an animal lives is its habitat. A polar bear's habitat is the frozen Arctic. A camel's habitat is a hot, dry desert.

Deep Ocean

Different animals live at different levels in the ocean. The deeper the water, the darker it is. Tuna and sea turtles live in the sunny top layer. Sperm whales and jellyfish live in deeper, darker water. Deep-sea anglerfish stay in the depths. Sponges and brittle stars live on the seafloor.

Deep-sea ribbonfish live in the ocean depths.

Rainforest Tree

Rainforests are hot and wet. They are home to more than half of the plants and animals on Earth. More than 3 million species live in the Amazon Rainforest. Rainforests are divided into layers, like the stories of a building. The top layer gets lots of sun. The layers get darker farther down. Different animals live in each layer.

RAINFOREST LAYERS

CANOPY

The treetops form a leafy roof called the canopy. Many birds, insects, and climbing animals live here.

UNDERSTORY

The understory is shaded from the sun by the canopy. Butterflies, snakes, and anteaters called tamanduas live in the understory.

FOREST FLOOR

The forest floor is dark. Jaguars, warthogs, and peccaries live down here.

Record Breakers

The world is full of record-breaking heights. The tallest man who ever lived was Robert Pershing Wadlow. He lived from 1918 to 1940. When he was last measured, he was 8 feet 11 inches (2.72 m) tall.

The world's tallest living tree is a giant redwood. It grows in California. The tree is nicknamed Hyperion. It measures an incredible 380 feet (115.8 m) tall!

FACT

At the age of 12, Robert Pershing Wadlow was already 6 feet 11 inches (2.10 m) tall.

The Empire State Building was the tallest building in the world when it was built in 1931. It held that record until 1971. The tallest building now is the Burj Khalifa in Dubai. It was finished in 2010. It measures 2,717 feet (828 m) tall.

The world's tallest mountain is Mount Everest, in the Himalayas. It is 29,035 feet (8,850 m) tall. The tallest mountain in the solar system is much, much taller. Mons Olympus is on the planet Mars. At 16 miles (24 km) high, it is three times higher than Mount Everest!

HANDS ON

Estimating Height

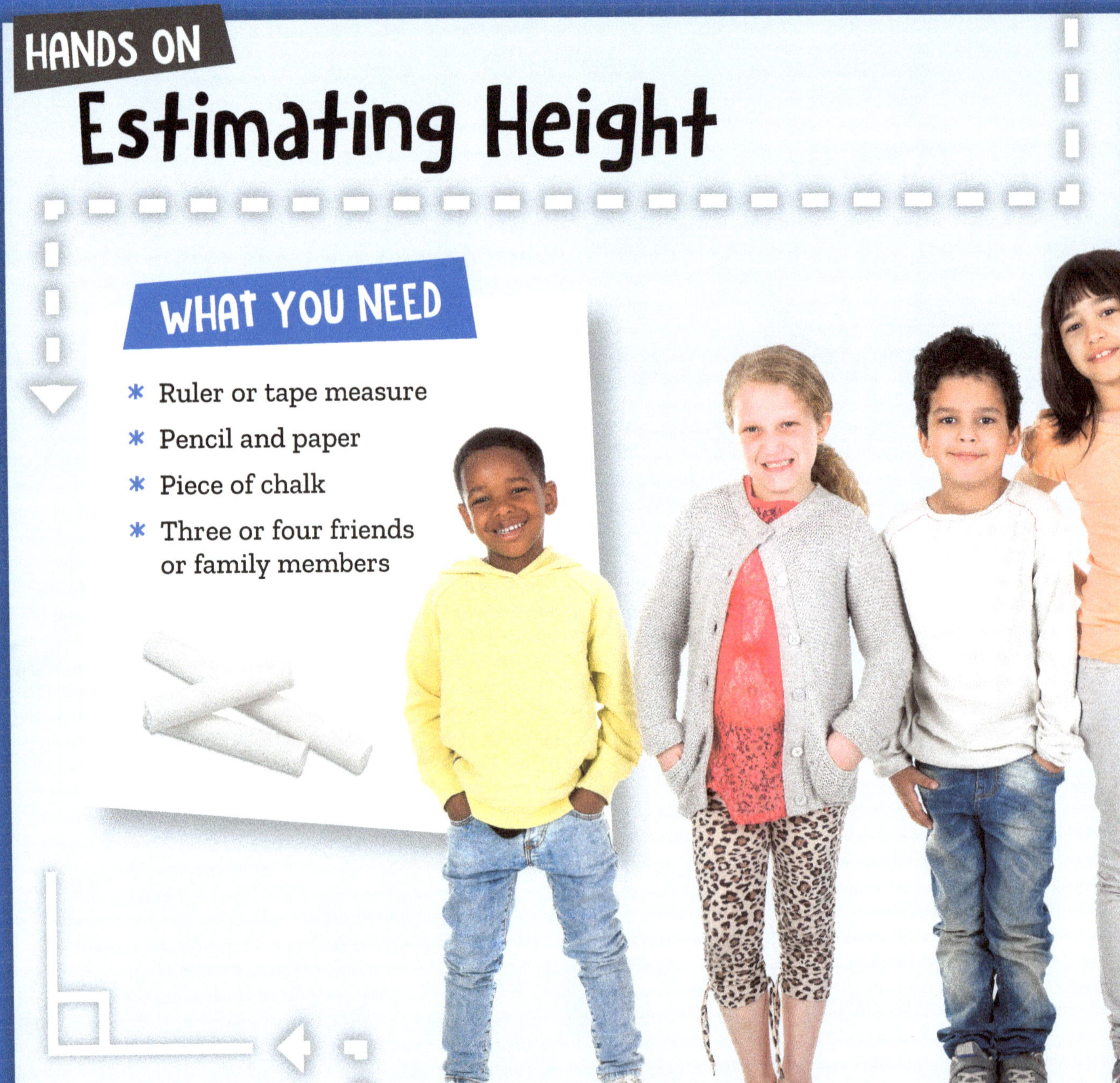

WHAT YOU NEED

* Ruler or tape measure
* Pencil and paper
* Piece of chalk
* Three or four friends or family members

WHAT YOU DO

1. Ask a friend to stand straight against a wall. Mark where the top of their head is on the wall with the chalk. Be careful not to damage the wall. Ask for permission first.

2. Measure from the ground to the mark. Write down the height on paper.

3. Look at the other people in your group. Are they taller or shorter than the person you just measured? How much taller or shorter?

4. Estimate each person's height. Write down what you think their height is.

5. Now measure their heights just as you did for the first person. Write the heights next to your estimates.

6. Were your estimates close? You should find that you get better and better at estimating as you go along.

Write the Units

When you write down a measurement, always put the units as well as the number. Your ruler or tape measure may be in inches, feet, centimeters, or meters. Make sure you write the unit as well as the number, so write 6 inches or 6 centimeters, not just "6."

Glossary

altimeter An instrument in an airplane that measures height.

altitude Height above sea level.

angle The space between two lines that cross or meet.

atmosphere The gases (air) we breathe that surround Earth.

centimeter A small distance equal to one meter divided by 100.

degree A unit for measuring angles.

depth Height that goes downward.

distance A measurement of the space between two points.

equator The imaginary line that runs around Earth's center.

estimate A rough calculation, better than a guess.

foot An imperial distance equal to 12 inches.

gravity A force that pulls things toward Earth.

height A distance between two points, measured upward.

imperial The system of measurements that is used in the United States. The imperial system is based on inches, feet, and yards.

inch An imperial distance.

length A distance measured sideways or along the ground.

meter A metric measurement equal to 3 feet 3 inches.

metric A set of measurements based on the meter.

navigation A way of finding a position on Earth, at sea, or in space.

protractor A device for measuring angles.

right angle A 90-degree angle.

ruler A straight measuring tool.

scale The marks on the side of a ruler, tape measure, or protractor.

scuba gear Air tank, face mask, wet suit, and flippers used for diving.

tape measure A long, flexible ruler.

yard An imperial distance equal to 3 feet.

Find Out More

BOOKS

Amstutz, Lisa J.
Rulers and Tape Measures.
Capstone Publishing, 2020.

Askew, Mike.
Let's Measure It
(You Can Master Math).
Rosen Publishing, 2022.

Celle, Clara.
How Many Flamingos Tall is a Giraffe?
Creative Ways to Look at Height.
Capstone Publishing, 2020.

Monster Math (four volumes).
Lerner Publishing, 2020.

WEBSITES

www.cuemath.com/measurement/
Convert lengths from imperial to metric units and from metric to imperial.

elementarymath.edc.org/resources/measurement-length-width-height-depth/
An introduction to measurement; length, width, height, and depth.

www.healthline.com/health/how-to-measure-height
How to measure the height of people, plus helpful links about height.

www.splashlearn.com/math-vocabulary/measurements/height
All about height, with illustrations and interactive games.

Index